AF334807

The Little House Who Didn't Lose Hope
Second Edition
is a heartwarming present- day parable for anyone of any age who
needs to be inspired and encouraged— especially those who have
felt abandoned, bullied, or hopeless. It also addresses the negative
consequences and effects that drug use can have on a family.

The Book is available in:
Hardcover, Paperback, PDF, and a coloring book.

Purchase at the WingMan Website
breakfreestayfree.com/books

Revenue generated through WingMan Books stays in the
WingMan program helping children recognize the pitfalls of addiction.

Also written by Nita Brady

The Dragonslayers Club is a fact-based story about
a special club where some students found out they were
not alone, could get the help they desperately needed,
and help each other as well.

Zeeko, The Bunny Who lost His Way
is a good introduction for young children (ages 6 to 10)
to understand the dangers of drugs and their negative consequences.

The Little House Who Didn't Lose Hope

Second Edition

by

Nita Brady

Illustrated by Ruth McKinsey

*This book is dedicated to children everywhere
who need to be encouraged to avoid
addictive substances.*

WELCOME TO
MAGNOLIA STREET

This is the story of a special little house on a street called Magnolia, in a place called Anytown, USA. Before I tell you about the little house, let me tell you about Magnolia Street. It was rightly called Magnolia Street because it had magnificent magnolia trees that lined both sides of the street, and because of that, there was much shade provided, which made it one of the most pleasant streets to walk on in Anytown, USA. There were also many lovely houses on Magnolia Street where grown-ups, children, dogs, and cats lived and played, and who enjoyed it very much.

The houses on Magnolia street were all unique – no two were alike. Some were large, some were small, some were quite formal, and some more simple. But they were all lovely with beautifully manicured lawns. All, that is, except one. And this is his story.

This house had lived on Magnolia Street for some time, and he stood out from all the rest. Why, you wonder? Was he nicer than the rest? More colorful? Bigger? Prettier yard? No. None of these. This little house stood out from all the rest because of his shabbiness, his ugliness. He was extremely rundown, with his paint peeling, his flower boxes cracked and rotten, his yard filled with dirt and weeds—Unlike all the others that had beautiful nice green lawns. He had a fence which at one time stood perfectly straight and tall. But now it leaned way over to one side. This only added to the rundown appearance of the little house.

And to make matters worse, some mean boys who lived in the houses across the street would always shout out bad names to the little house, and throw rocks at his windows until they were cracked and broken. But those boys weren't the only ones who bullied and mocked the little house. The houses that the boys lived in picked up this bad behavior and joined in, especially the two large fancy mansion-style houses across the street. They were the worst!

"Just look at him," one of the large houses would call out to the other. "Why, he is a total disgrace!" "He sure is," the other house would agree. "He really belongs in the dump." Hey, that's a perfect name for him--Dumpy!" and they'd yell this ugly name out to him again and again. "Any day now they're going to come with a wrecking ball and cart your shabby parts off to the dump! Ha ha! We can't wait! You're an eyesore, that's what you are! Dumpy the Eyesore, Dumpy the Eyesore!" they chanted over and over.

The little house tried to ignore this taunting but sometimes it was so hard. Especially when he thought about the times when he wasn't so ugly and shabby-looking. When he thought about those times when his family lived there, the tears began to roll down his walls and he thought he might just die from the pain of it all. When the two big mean houses across the street saw his tear-stained walls, this made them mock him even more. "Hey Dumpy, now you look even worse! What a loser you are! Hey I think I hear that wrecking ball!" And then they would laugh in the meanest way.

MERRY CHRISTMAS
WELCOME
PEACE

No, the little house hadn't always been this way. He thought back to the times when the children in the family played games on his lush lawn. He remembered when the mother planted a garden in the backyard—how the family enjoyed the vegetable plants and flowers! And when Christmas came, they decorated him so nicely with brightly colored lights, they put a holly wreath on his door, mistletoe on the top of his doorways, and a beautiful Christmas tree that everyone could see from his front window. And he loved to hear the family talking about what they called "The Christmas Story," about how a baby named Jesus came into the world, born in a manger, in a stable where animals lived, of all wasn't places! The children would ask again and again why this One who created the world and everything in it, was born in such a place, and not in a palace. The mother would just smile and say that when Jesus came, He was God's gift for all people—rich or poor—He was love coming down from heaven. The little house didn't fully understand all of those things, but he loved to hear the story and see how happy it made his family.

Yes, those were grand times! Times when the family would gather around the dinner table and laugh, and the children would tell stories of their times at school. Oh what love was shared around their table!

But his very favorite times were when the family gathered to work—on him! They polished his floors, cleaned his walls, swept his kitchen, cleaned his bathrooms, swept his front porch, mowed his lawn, and watered the flowers in his flower boxes. He loved it when his family took such great care of him and made him shine!

And then one day—they were gone. It was a very sad and confusing day
when they left. He had heard a lot of crying and yelling the night before, and
a lot of rushing around and slamming his doors! And then the police came,
and they took the father away! He didn't understand what in the world was
happening! But he remembered hearing the mother shouting something about
a word he had never heard before—drugs. And as the police were taking the
father away, the mother cried out to him, "Oh, how could you do this to us?" The
children were crying, too, and it made the little house sad and afraid. Whatever
this thing called "drugs" was, it must be very bad! It was causing a lot of sadness
and confusion and fear.

The next day, the little house watched the family. He saw the boy with an
angry look on his face, his arms crossed, his head down. His sister was crying
and saying, "Why do we have to move? I love this house!" But her mother just
hugged her and said, "I'm so sorry, darling. We just have to go. Someday, you'll

understand." Then a big truck showed up and all their furniture got hauled away.

He would never forget that first night after the family was gone. It was so dark and so quiet, and so sad. No one to gather at the table, no one to play on his lawn. No one playing on his floors. And he began to cry. First a little trickle came, then buckets of tears flowed and filled up the flower boxes outside his front windows.

"There, there," the flowers tried to comfort him. "They'll be back." But they didn't come back. That thing called "drugs" really messed everything up!

Then the mean houses across the street made him feel even worse when they called over to him, "Ha Ha! We saw everything. Your owner is a jailbird now! What a loser! They'll never come back! And you're a loser, too!"

Days turned to months, months turned to years. The rains came and beat against his walls. The heat came and dried up his lawn, turning it an ugly brown.

The little house began to get shabbier and shabbier. And uglier and uglier. And the taunting and the mocking of the big houses grew louder and louder.

But there was one bright spot in his sad life. It was the sweet house next door. She wasn't large and fancy like the houses across the street, but she was very well kept up, her yards mowed, flowers lining her walkway, always cheerful, always clean. But what made her the most attractive was her kindness. She always had an encouraging word for him. "Don't listen to those mean ol' houses," she would say. "Your heart is still beautiful, and that's the most important thing of all. Don't give up. Keep hoping, Little House. Any day now, something good is going to happen, I just know it! In fact, I pray every night and every morning that God will send you a new family to love you."

"You do?" the little house asked.

"Yes, I do. So don't despair. Don't lose hope. I believe. So, you believe, too, ok?" The little house thought about this a long time. He remembered the things his family had said about God, how He loved everyone. Maybe even a shabby, ugly little house like him. These kind words from his friend encouraged him and gave him hope. Maybe she was right. Maybe he shouldn't give up. Maybe he, too, should pray for a new family. And he did. Night and day he prayed. Time passed. The taunts and insults across the street continued. But the little house did not give up hope.

814
WELCOME
FRIENDS

And then one day…everything changed. Some people came to his door. Who could this be? No one ever came to his door. But one of them had a key and they slowly opened his front door. It creaked loudly as no one had opened his door for so long. Two children, a man, and woman were with the person who had the key. The children walked around wide-eyed, and the little boy said, "This house is creepy. Why are we looking at it?" And the man agreed. "Let's get out of here," he said disgustedly. "We're wasting our time here. This place is a dump." And the little house wanted to cry out, "No no, I'm not creepy! I'm not a dump! I've just been neglected because my family left me! Please stay! Oh, won't you please stay!" But he knew they would not be able to hear him, for only houses can hear each other.

But then the mother of the children, who had been wandering through the little house, opening doors and looking around, stopped and said, "Wait, let's not leave yet, let's stay just a little longer. There is something that feels very, very familiar about this house, something about the way it's built. It reminds me so much of the house that I grew up in, just a few streets over, on Sycamore Street. And just look at this lovely street, with all the beautiful magnolia trees…it's such a nice neighborhood."

The little house had been listening very closely to this conversation. "Sycamore Street!" he thought. "Oh my goodness, my mother lived on Sycamore Street!" Could it really be possible...? Did this kind lady live in the house that was his mother? Did she play and laugh within his mother's walls and play in her backyard when she was a child?

"I think all it needs is some TLC," she said.

"TLC?" the little house wondered. "What is this TLC that the lady thinks I need?"

"This house needs more than TLC—and it would cost a lot of money," the man replied.

Then the lady answered, "Well, it would cost much more to buy a new house, wouldn't it?"

Just then, the boy who had wandered into the backyard while his parents were talking, came bursting back into the house. "Mom! Dad! Come look outside at the backyard! It's HUGE! And it looks like somebody built a fort back here, too! It's really cool! Come on, you've got to see it!"

The parents smiled, then walked outside and looked at the great big backyard. When they saw their children playing happily, they looked at each other. The father rubbed his chin and said, "Well, maybe you're right. Maybe we could get some friends and family to help us, because it's going to take a LOT of TLC. He turned to the lady with the key, "OK, I guess we'll take it," he said. His wife smiled and his children jumped up and down, clapping their hands and laughing.

"They'll take me! They'll take me!" the little house thought excitedly. He wanted to sing and dance and cry for joy. Then suddenly he thought, "Well, I guess I'll find out what this TLC is. I hope it doesn't hurt too much or last too long. But they want me! They want me! Even with all my shabbiness and ugliness--they want me!" Then he remembered what the kind house next door had told him, to never give up hope, to keep believing, keep praying. He felt joy running through his floorboards, his walls, his ceiling as he turned his windows up towards heaven. "You heard me! You DO care, even about a shabby little house like me!" And this time he cried tears of joy.

Just then the mean boys came running out of their mean houses. "Hey, I saw some people looking at that dump across the street, did you see them?"

KID'S CLUB

"Yeah, I did," the other mean boy answered. But who in the world would want that ugly, disgusting house? They're probably making plans to tear it down!"

So, of course the mean houses joined in, trying to dampen the spirit of the little house. "Oh, SURE, they want you! Why would they want you, Dumpy! I heard they looked at my grand cousin on Vine Street. I'm sure they'll pick him over you! Dumpy Eyesore, Dumpy Eyesore!" they taunted him. "Nobody wants you…I'm sure I hear the wrecking ball this time!"

But their words could not hurt the little house this time. He was full of joy, and for the first time, he actually felt sorry for these mean houses. They had nothing good or kind of joyful or hopeful about them. He looked right at them and he said, "You're wrong. That family does want me, you'll see. And you know what, I forgive you for saying those things to me. Your words will not hurt me any longer. I feel sorry for you."

The mean houses stood silent for a moment. They looked at each other, then back at the shabby house, and said, "YOU feel sorry for us? That's ridiculous!"

Just then, a girl came out of the house next door. She was always sweet and kind, just like her house, who was always so encouraging and kind to the little shabby house. "I heard what you said," she told the boys. "You just never know. Maybe that family does want to buy him, and make him their new home. All it would take is some TLC."

Then the sweet house called over to the mean houses. "Why don't you two just pipe down!" she scolded. "Don't you ever have anything nice to say?" Then she turned to the little house and fluttered her shutters. "I'm so happy for you! I just knew you would get a family someday. They're going to give you lots of TLC and it will be just grand!"

There it was again. TLC. What in the world was this TLC? So, he asked the kind house and she quietly, mysteriously said, "Oh, you'll find out soon enough. Just you wait and see!" When she said this she could hardly contain her joy.

We All
Need
TLC

So the day finally came. His new family came back, and brought lots and lots of friends and family members with them. They carried all kinds of cleaning supplies and equipment and hammers and nails and paint—and they all pitched in and worked together for many days. The little house was so happy to hear all the talking and laughing and joking. He just couldn't stop smiling. He wondered if his new family could somehow see his smile or feel his happiness!

At the end of the week, so much had been accomplished. The friends all left and the family stood in front of their little house to admire all their hard work. The little house had a new paint job, new flower boxes full of flowers, new floors, a new roof, new windows, and even a new lawn! "I declare," the mother said. "It looks like this little house is smiling!" So, they could see it! That made him even happier!

"Well," the father answered, "you were right, Dear. All this house really needed was some TLC: tender loving care." He smiled and said, "Now let's go in and make it something more than a house, let's make it our home!"

So that was it! TLC—it stood for Tender Loving Care! Outside under his two front windows, two tears dropped down onto the new flowers in the flower boxes. The little tulips raised their heads and said, "Little House, why are you crying? You aren't dumpy any more. The family's TLC has completely transformed you! You're beautiful!"

"I know," the little house said as he smiled through his tears. "I'm just so happy." He thought many thoughts then, about how God saw him and cared for him, even when he was still dumpy….and how He had heard the cries of his little shabby house heart…how he didn't give up hope, how he believed God would send him a new family. And He did. Surely, God must have been the Creator of this TLC. Then he thought about his first family, about that terrible thing called "drugs" that messed everything up and upset the family so much. He hoped the father was doing better, and that the family found a new house to love them like he did. He knew what he had to do, right then and there. He lifted up

his windows to the sky, and he said a prayer for his old family, that God would send them all some TLC, help them, and give them some hope.

Time passed, and then one day the little house noticed a car drop off a girl in front of the kind house next door. Something about her looked familiar…. She knocked on the front door, and then the kind girl came out of her house. The little house listened closely to their conversation. As he listened his windows grew a little larger, and he thought, "No wonder she looks familiar! It's the girl who used to live here!"

"Well, things are better now," he heard her say. "We live in a house across town. It's not as nice as our house we used to live in next door, but it's ok."

Her kind friend looked down and softly asked, "How is your dad, Tiffany?" The little house took a deep breath. He was almost afraid to hear what she would say. But he leaned in a bit so he could hear a little better. He had to know.

She smiled a sad little smile. "Well, he's still in prison…but he's doing better. He writes to me, and sometimes he draws pictures, and sends them to me. He says he's sorry for the choices he made, and he's going to do better. I hope so."

Her kind friend, whose name was Juliet, gave her a hug, and said, "Oh, Tiffany, I hope so, too.

Tiffany looked down and shyly said, "There's something else that's been helping me a lot, too."

"Really?" Juliet's eyes grew wide. "What?"

Tiffany answered, smiling. "Well, I've been going to this special support group."

"What's a support group?" Juliette asked.

"It's a group of other students who are...well, going through basically the same thing I'm going through. And we help each other. I've made some new friends there, too," Tiffany said.

Juliette smiled a big smile. "That sounds really good, Tiffany! A special support group. Wow, that sounds totally cool. I'm so happy for you!"

The girls hugged, and then Juliette said, "Want to come in and hang out in my room? I've got some cool stuff I want to show you!"

As the girls went inside, the kind house called over to the little house. "Did you hear that, Little House? There's always hope. We just can't give up!"

"You're right! We can't lose hope. I've been praying that God would send my old family some TLC….looks like He did!" And Tiffany's getting help, and it sounds like her dad is doing better!"

Then suddenly the mean houses across the street called out, "Hey! Just because you got a little paint, don't think you're all that! You're STILL dumpy! And we're still bigger and grander than you are! You'll never be as nice and beautiful as we are! Hmmmmph!"

But the little house just kept smiling. Their words didn't bother him at all. Then the kind house next door who had heard these mean comments said, "You two never learn, do you? Just pipe down, no one wants to hear you." So, they just sat and pouted because they didn't want to admit that all of that TLC made the little house quite stunning. And nearly every day, everyone who walked down Magnolia Street took notice of him, saying things like, "Oh, wow, look at that one! It really stands out, doesn't it? What a beautiful house! Why, it even looks like it's smiling!"

"TLC", the little house sighed, "what a wonderful thing it is that God made!" And he began to think more thoughts. "What would happen," he pondered, "if every man, woman, child, animal, plant, and house could ALL experience God's TLC and hope? And what if they shared it with others? What a different world it would be…"

Yes, indeed, what a different world it would be!

20

Discussion Questions:

- How did the little house get so shabby and ugly?
- What did he love about his first family?
- Who made a bad choice in the story? What were the consequences?
- How were others affected by the bad choice?
- Who was mean to the little house?
- Has anyone ever been mean to you?
- Who showed kindness in the story?
- What advice did the kind house give to the little house?
- How did the little house respond when he found out he was going to have a new family?
- What are you thankful for in your life?
- How did the little house find out what TLC was? Who said what it meant?
- According to the little house, who created TLC?
- Have you ever experienced TLC? Have you shared it with anyone else?
- Do you believe this would be a better world if everyone experienced TLC and never lost hope?
- Who or what will help us to make good choices in life?

WingMan

The WingMan book program has been created for children of all ages.
We realize that children are being exposed to addictive substances at
younger ages every year.

Our goal is to prevent addiction by creating awareness and crafting
stories and images that are fun as well as informative.

If we can save a single child from destroying his or her life
we will consider our efforts a success.

CPSIA information can be obtained
at www.ICGtesting.com
Printed in the USA
LVHW070757130920
664725LV00057B/2080